I AM
She
WHO IS
VALUABLE

An Inclusive Spiritual Care Guide
for Self-love and Empowerment

I AM She WHO IS VALUABLE

SHEVALLE T. KIMBER, M.DIV.

ISBN: 978-1-957621-77-7

*Empowering You
to Thrive through
Life's Challenges*

I AM

She

WHO IS SMART!

Table of Contents

I AM

She

WHO IS ENOUGH!

Preface

Understanding the value of women in today's world is essential, especially given the societal and cultural challenges we face. Many women (regardless of age, background, or culture) struggle with self-worth due to external pressures, unrealistic beauty standards, and gender inequality. This study is designed to affirm our God-given value—fostering confidence, healing, and a deeper awareness of how God sees us and how we should view ourselves, rather than our allowing the world to define us.

Whether you are exploring this material individually, in a small group, or in a classroom setting, these teachings offer encouragement and insight. By reinforcing the importance of women's leadership and worth, we can counter misconceptions that have historically limited women's roles in both society and faith communities. Women are vital to our families, ministries, and broader communities.

Through this study, you will find affirmation, practical wisdom, and empowerment to grow spiritually, strengthen your confidence, and step boldly into your God-given purpose—regardless of cultural expectations. Whether learning alone at home or engaging in group discussions, may this journey deepen your understanding and inspire transformation in your life.

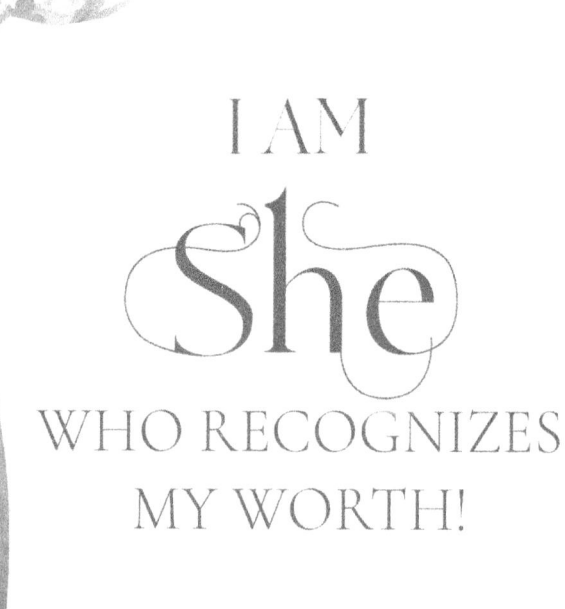

I AM

She

WHO RECOGNIZES

MY WORTH!

Introduction

I Am She Who Is Valuable is a transformative and inclusive manual designed to guide individuals—particularly women—in cultivating self-love, self-care, and empowerment through an interfaith, spiritual framework. Rooted in the belief that each person is inherently valuable, this book empowers participants to navigate life's inevitable struggles (whether in school, at work, or in relationships or society) by building strong, supportive practices for personal growth, stress management, and emotional well-being.

The manual combines reflective journaling, group discussions, and creative activities to help participants discover their passions and develop rituals for sustaining their journey of self-discovery. It offers a holistic approach to self-care by addressing emotional, mental, physical, and spiritual well-being while fostering community, healing, and resilience. This manual begins with five reflections designed to inspire and guide the reader in thinking creatively about the wisdom embodied by women. I hope each one of these helps women to embrace their inherent personal value and the communal value in functioning with other women. Following the reflections are ten practical principles of wisdom for growth. The last section of the book contains the objectives, modules, and lessons for a journey of self-discovery. You can use this portion of the book as a group curriculum or for your personal use. The choice is yours. It is my sincere prayer that this book is a blessing to you!

I AM She
WHO IS STRENGTH!

PART 1

I Am SHE Who Is Valuable ~ She Who Is You, She Who Is Me:
A Reflection on Wisdom, Strength, and the Divine Feminine

Beloveds,

As we embark on this journey of recognizing and honoring our intrinsic worth, it is essential to embrace a few fundamental truths—insights that have transformed the way I perceive my value and that of others. Life has shown me that across cultures, races, and religions, a woman's worth is often measured by external standards: beauty, success, wealth, or the roles we fulfill. However, beneath these surface-level markers lies a deeper, more profound truth—one woven into the very fabric of our existence.

In my search for wisdom, I turned to the Scriptures . . . and Proverbs 3:15-18 stood out: *"Wisdom is more precious than jewels; nothing you desire can compare with her. She offers long life in her right hand, and wealth and honor in her left. Her ways are pleasant, and all her paths lead to peace. She is a tree of life to those who embrace her; those who hold her tight are truly happy."* (paraphrase)

This passage reveals a reality that transcends time and culture: wisdom is life-giving, more valuable than anything we could seek. More strikingly, wisdom is personified as *She.*

King Solomon, revered as the wisest man of his time, lived in an era when women had little agency . . . with their worth defined by men. And yet, he named wisdom *She.* Imagine that—wisdom, one of the most precious of all virtues—is *She.*

For this book, *She* represents you and me. As we walk and breathe, divine wisdom lives within us—not as a distant, intangible concept, but as a force woven into our very being. While Solomon may not have intended the feminine pronoun literally, his words serve as a powerful reminder that women embody wisdom through our strength, resilience, and intuition.

So, as we uncover the many ways that we are inherently valuable, I invite you to look beyond external measures and embrace the wisdom that dwells within. For *She*—the wisdom of God—is alive in each of us.

I AM
She
WHO BELIEVES!

The Wisdom of SHE

Beloveds,

When we read Proverbs 3:15-18, we encounter a striking image—of a woman more precious than jewels, whose hands hold both long life and honor. Her paths are peaceful, and those who embrace her are called blessed. This woman is not just a poetic ideal or an abstract concept. She is alive. She is present. She is *you*. She is *me*. She is wisdom.

Wisdom and women are inseparable—woven together as intimately as the color of our skin, as intrinsic as breath itself. Yet, wisdom is not a prize to be won or a commodity to be measured by the world's standards. It is not found in perfection but in presence—in the way we live with intention, navigate hardship, and hold space for ourselves and others. Wisdom is not only something we acquire; it is something we carry, nurture, and pass on—just as women have always done, often in silence, often unseen.

For centuries, women have embodied wisdom in many forms—as mothers, daughters, sisters, and friends. And though society may try to diminish or overlook the value of women's contributions, the wisdom we carry is undeniable. It exists not just in what we do, but in *how* we do it—in our resilience, creativity, and ability to balance the weight of the world while still holding on to ourselves.

Even when we go unnoticed, we persist.

We *are* wisdom. We are *She*. And we are invaluable.

Notes

_____

_____

_____

_____

I AM

She

WHO CAN DO
WHATEVER I SET
MY MIND TO DO!

The Legacy of Wisdom: Eve and the Divine Feminine

Let us take a moment to reflect on the first woman in the Bible: Eve. Genesis 3:20 tells us, *"Adam called his wife's name Eve, because she was the mother of all living"* (NKJV). As the first woman created, Eve was not only the mother of humanity but also the mother of wisdom. Though she was the first to walk the path of womanhood—with no guide to follow, no mother, grandmother, aunties or homegirls to teach her, and no societal framework to shape her role—she carried within her the wisdom that would sustain generations to come.

Eve's story is powerful because she stepped into the unknown and became the first to navigate the complexities of life. She experienced love, loss, trial, and transformation—all without precedent. In doing so, she embodied the resilience, strength, and wisdom that we, as women, continue to inherit today.

Just as Eve carried wisdom in a world that was new to her, so do we. Women are born with an innate capacity for wisdom—an ability to adapt, to endure, and to thrive. This wisdom is not something to be measured or confined by traditional understanding. It is meant to be *lived*, *felt*, and *shared*. As I often tell my sons, *"Women think of things you can't even fathom."* This is not because women are mysterious, but because wisdom itself is vast, evolving, and deeply rooted in experience.

Wisdom is not simply something we possess—it is something we are. It is alive in us, just as it was in Eve.

Notes

_____

_____

_____

_____

I AM

She

WHO IS STRONG!

She Who Is You and Me Is Valuable

It's easy to feel invisible, misunderstood, or undervalued in a world that often measures worth by superficial standards—beauty, success, productivity. Yet, Proverbs reminds us that *wisdom is more precious than jewels.* The wisdom carried within women cannot be measured by fleeting ideals. It is deeper, richer, and far more enduring. When you look in the mirror today, see beyond what the world tells you to value. See the wisdom within you. Say it with me: *"I am she. She who is me is valuable."*

Every woman you encounter, whether at the grocery store, in the workplace, or waiting at the bus stop, is valuable. She is a living testament to the wisdom of God, carrying a story woven with growth, struggle, and triumph. And in carrying her story, she carries wisdom. Let us not judge one another by what we see on the surface. Instead, let us honor the divine wisdom that resides within each woman. Whether we realize it or not, we all have something to teach, something to share . . . something to pass on.

Value is not determined by external validation but by the quiet strength that endures through every trial. It is in the mother soothing her child after a long day, the young woman pushing through self-doubt to chase her dreams, the grandmother whose words carry the weight of decades of experience. You are not just what you do or how you look—you are the sum of all the love you have given, all the lessons you have learned, and all the wisdom you have yet to share. When you uplift another woman, when you recognize her worth, you reflect the truth that has always been: *she who is me, she who is you, is valuable.*

Notes

_____

_____

_____

_____

I AM

She

WHO IS LOVED!

Lessons from "The Color Purple": Wisdom in Community

My favorite movie of all time is *The Color Purple* (Alice Walker, *The Color Purple*. Harcourt, 1982). This film is more than just a cinematic masterpiece—it is the bedrock of liberation, a story that speaks to the soul of every woman who has ever felt unseen, unheard, or undervalued across the spans of age. *The Color Purple* is not just about survival; it is about the reclamation of self, the realization of worth, and the transformative power of love and wisdom.

Nettie, through her love, strength, and guidance, teaches her older sister, Celie, not just how to survive but how to reclaim her worth and embrace life fully. She does not guard her wisdom selfishly; instead, she pours it into Celie, even when Celie feels broken and unseen. In that exchange, wisdom becomes a bridge—connecting, healing, and empowering.

What makes this movie so powerful is the way it measures value, not by wealth, beauty, or social status, but by the resilience, love, and wisdom carried by the women featured . . . not just Celie and her sister, Nettie, but Shug and Sofia as well. They all embody different forms of strength, and through their struggles, we see that true value lies in the ability to endure, uplift, and love fiercely.

These relationships offer us a powerful truth that wisdom is not meant to be kept to ourselves but to be shared. As women, we are called both to carry wisdom and to pass it on—to uplift, support, and celebrate one another. Just as Nettie uplifted Celie, we, must rise up together and be strengthened.

Notes

_____

_____

_____

_____

I AM

She

WHO CAN BE
WHATEVER I WANT
TO BE!

PART 2

Practical Wisdom for Loving God, Yourself, and Your Community

As you consider the importance of wisdom in your life, here are ten practical steps to help you love God, yourself, and your community:

- **Recognize Your Worth:** You are inherently valuable, not by society's standards but through the boundless love of God.

- **Embrace Your Path:** Every experience—joyful or challenging—is part of your divine journey. Trust in your growth, healing, and transformation.

- **Uplift Others:** Share your wisdom, kindness, and strength with the women around you. Empower, encourage, and support one another.

- **Love Yourself Fiercely:** Embrace yourself fully—your beauty, your flaws, and your power—just as God loves you unconditionally.

- **Strengthen Your Community:** Use your gifts to uplift those around you, creating a foundation of love, support, and unity.

- **Be Fearless:** Face your struggles with courage and resilience. Don't let fear keep you from stepping into your purpose.

- **Share Your Truth:** Your story has the power to inspire and heal. Speak it boldly, knowing that it can light the way for others.

- **Protect Your Peace:** Set boundaries that honor your well-being. Saying "no" when necessary is an act of self-care and self-respect.

- **Live in the Moment:** In a world full of distractions, choose to be fully present—with yourself, your loved ones, and your purpose.

- **Honor the Wisdom Within:** Trust the divine wisdom that resides in you. Live it, share it, and let it guide you every day.

Notes

I AM

She

WHO IS RESILIENT!

Learning Outcomes:

1. **Empowerment through Self-Care:** Develop practical strategies for managing stress and improving overall health.

2. **Building Resilience:** Cultivate the inner strength to face adversity and remain positive.

3. **Nurturing Relationships:** Learn how to communicate effectively, set boundaries, and build a support network.

4. **Self-discovery and Spirituality:** Engage in personal reflection and embrace the journey of self-love and transformation.

Notes

_____

_____

_____

_____

_____

_____

_____

_____

_____

I AM
She
WHO IS BRAVE!

Module Breakdown

Module 1: Introduction to Self-care

Scripture: Proverbs 4:23 (CEB)
"More than anything you guard, protect your mind, for life flows from it."

Lesson 1: Understanding Self-care

- **Objective:** Define what self-care is to you and explore its significance in fostering emotional, mental, and spiritual well-being. Example: *Taking my dog for a few short walks throughout the day not only gets my body moving and blood flowing but also helps me reset after a meeting. This behavior contributes to my overall well-being.* It is a form of self-care.

  _____

  _____

  _____

  _____

- **Interactive Activity:** *Self-care Reflection Worksheet*
  List your current self-care habits and evaluate their impact on various aspects of your life. Encourage sharing in small groups.

  _____

  _____

  _____

  _____

- **Discussion Prompt:** How do we define "self-care" in the context of our faith and daily life? Example: *I set a reminder on my phone to*

*pray at 10:00 a.m. No matter where I am or what I am doing, praying
centers my day and sets the tone for the remainder of it.*

_____

_____

_____

_____

- **Outcome:** This activity should leave you with a clear definition of
  self-care and an understanding of its foundational importance.

_____

_____

_____

_____

Lesson 2: Types of Self-care

- **Objective:** Explore the varied dimensions of self-care: physical,
  emotional, mental, social, and spiritual. Keep in mind that self-
  care looks different for everyone. Example: *One person may find
  relaxation in a manicure, while another may unwind with a cup of
  tea before bed, a candlelit bath, a cooking class, or a therapy session.
  Ultimately, self-care is anything that feels right, recenters your soul,
  and brings clarity to your thoughts.*

_____

_____

_____

_____

- **Activity:** *Create a Self-care Wheel*
  This is a visual chart dividing a circle into different segments that represent types of self-care, which include but are not limited to physical, emotional, social, mental, spiritual, environmental, and/or financial aspects.

- **Discussion:** Share practical examples of activities for each type of self-care. Example: *A manicure embodies both the physical and mental aspects of self-care. It involves the tangible touch and treatment of the nails and hands. It enhances your appearance while also fostering a sense of well-being and confidence—reflecting the mental side of self-care.*

  _____

  _____

  _____

  _____

Module 2: Assessing Your Needs

Scripture: Psalm 139:23 (KJV)
"Search me, O God, and know my heart; try me and know my thoughts."

Lesson 1: *Self-assessment*

- **Objective:** Conduct a self-assessment to evaluate strengths and areas of improvement in each dimension of self-care.

  _____

  _____

  _____

  _____

- **Interactive Activity:** *Life Assessment Inventory*
  Create a checklist of questions that prompt reflection on your emotional, mental, physical, social, and spiritual needs. You will score yourself to evaluate in which areas you may need to improve. Example questions: *Are you grateful today? Have you been kind to yourself today? Have you spoken kind words to yourself? Has anyone offended you this week? How did it make you feel?* (Answer each question, attempting to rate each response 1-5.)

  _____

  _____

  _____

  _____

- **Discussion:** Reflect on the assessment results in pairs, small groups, or alone.

  _____

  _____

  _____

Lesson 2: *Identifying Barriers to Self-care*

- **Objective:** Identify common obstacles to practicing self-care, such as time management, guilt, and external pressures. Examples: *Failing to prepare your gym bag the night before is poor time management because it results in being late for work. Feeling guilty about doing something nice for yourself, such as buying a new dress or an ice cream cone. External pressures can arise from family and friends, often leading you to prioritize their needs over your own.*

- **Activity:** *Barrier Brainstorming Session*
  Work alone or in small groups to share and brainstorm solutions to common barriers to self-care.

  _____

  _____

  _____

  _____

- **Discussion:** How can we create spaces in our lives to prioritize self-care despite external pressures?

  _____

  _____

  _____

  _____

Module 3: Creating Your Self-care Plan

Scripture: Matthew 6:33 (NKJV)
"But seek first the kingdom of God and His righteousness, and all these things will be added to you."

Lesson 1: *Setting SMART Goals*

- **Objective:** Set specific, measurable, achievable, relevant, and time-bound (SMART) self-care goals.

_____

_____

_____

_____

- **Activity:** *Goal Setting Workshop*
Write down one specific self-care goal for each dimension of self-care (physical, emotional, mental, social, spiritual). Example: *A smart goal I have for myself is to take daily walks. I carve out thirty-five (35) minutes in the morning and afternoon. I measure it using a walking app on my smartphone. Another example is planned reading time or television time. Additionally, I have a worry time. If I am going to worry about anything, I give it five minutes of my day and move on. This way, I don't allow my day to be wasted on worry.*

_____

_____

_____

_____

- **Reflection:** Discuss how setting intentional goals can align with your faith and spiritual journey.

_____

_____

_____

Lesson 2: *Developing a Personalized Self-care Plan*

- **Objective:** Create a tailored self-care plan based on your needs and goals.

_____

_____

_____

_____

- **Activity:** *My Self-care Blueprint*
Create a weekly and monthly self-care routine, integrating practices that resonate with you.

EXAMPLE: <u>MY SELF-CARE PLAN FOR THE WEEK</u>

MONDAY–FRIDAY
- *Morning walk, morning coffee, morning bubble bath, fruit, then off to work.*
- *Afternoon walk, lunch break, or yoga class.*
- *In the evenings, I prepare dinner and watch my favorite weekly shows on Wednesday and Thursday evenings. Reading and journaling on Mondays and Fridays.*

SATURDAY
- *Planting, riding my bike, and hanging out with family and friends.*

SUNDAY
- *Church, brunch with family, and Sunday dinner with family followed by a card game.*

- **Discussion:** How can we stay flexible and adaptable in our self-care routines, understanding that life is ever-changing? My life experiences have taught me to stay flexible and adaptable with my self-care routines and to view challenges that arise as opportunities for growth. Life is constantly evolving, so embracing change and remaining open to new ideas is essential. Additionally, staying curious and asking thoughtful questions can provide clarity, helping us adjust our self-care practices to fit our ever-changing needs.

_____

_____

_____

Module 4: Self-care Practices

Scripture: Matthew 6:34a (ESV)
"Therefore do not be anxious about tomorrow, for tomorrow will be anxious for itself."

Lesson 1: *Mindfulness and Meditation*

- **Objective:** Introduce mindfulness techniques and the benefits of meditation for emotional regulation and stress reduction. Mindfulness is focused moment awareness. In other words, be wholly present during your meditation, however you define it. Example: *My mindful meditations are my walks. I walk in silence, praying to God and reflecting on life while paying attention to my steps and breathing. I also listen to the sounds of nature and the world around me.*

_____

_____

_____

- **Activity:** *Guided Mindfulness Practice*
  Engage in a two- to five-minute mindfulness meditation, focusing on breathing and presence. Example: *Sit with your eyes closed and focus on your breathing. Clear your head.*

- **Discussion:** How can mindfulness connect us to the present moment and to God's presence in our lives?

  _____

  _____

  _____

  _____

- **Reflection:** Share how mindfulness can reduce anxiety and increase self-awareness.

  _____

  _____

  _____

  _____

Lesson 2: *Relaxation Techniques*

- **Objective:** Teach relaxation exercises, including deep breathing, progressive muscle relaxation, and visualization.

- **Activity:** *Guided Relaxation Session*
  Practice progressive muscle relaxation and visualization techniques. Example: *While sitting or lying down, breathe deeply, and tense muscles from feet to toes, then legs, thighs, buttocks, stomach, back, arms, and hands, releasing each with each breath.*

- **Discussion:** How can these techniques be integrated into daily routines for stress management?

  _____

  _____

_____

_____

Module 5: Stress Management

Scripture: Philippians 4:6 (ESV)
"Do not be anxious about anything, but in everything by prayer and supplication with thanksgiving let your requests be made known to God."

Lesson 1: *Understanding Stress*

- **Objective:** Examine the physiological (bodily functions) and psychological (mental and emotional) effects of stress and identify common sources.

_____

_____

_____

_____

- **Interactive Activity:** *Stress Mapping*
Map out your primary stressors and share coping strategies, either individually or in groups. Example: *Write your name in the center of a page. Then, draw a circle and a line to represent what causes you stress, the level of stress, and how they are all interconnected.*

- **Discussion:** How does stress impact our minds, bodies, and spirits, and how can faith help us find peace in times of stress?

_____

_____

_____

_____

Lesson 2: *Coping Strategies*

- **Objective:** Introduce effective coping strategies, such as problem solving, time management, and seeking social support.

_____

_____

_____

_____

- **Activity:** *Stress Management Role-play*
  Alone or in pairs, you will role-play a stressful situation and practice applying one coping mechanism that has been discussed.

- **Reflection:** Discuss how we can rely on God's guidance to help us manage stress in a healthy way.

_____

_____

_____

_____

Module 6: Building Resilience

Scripture: 2 Corinthians 4:8 (NIV)
We are hard pressed on every side, but not crushed; perplexed, but not in despair.

Lesson 1: *Resilience Skills*

- **Objective:** Define what *resilience* means to you and explore techniques for cultivating it. One such way is to reframe negative thoughts and find meaning in adversity. I define resilience as the ability never to give up. Eleanor Roosevelt said, "Do the thing you think you cannot do." So, instead of saying to yourself or allowing anyone else to tell you to give up because it's not worth it or because you've tried and failed, turn all those thoughts into positives that say, "I am *She* who is valuable, and I can do it!"

  _____

  _____

  _____

- **Activity:** *Resilience Mapping*
  Identify a personal challenge you've overcome and map out the resilience-building techniques you used. You will draw a circle on a blank sheet of paper and then draw a line connecting it to the next circle or square in the challenge, indicating how you have overcome it. Example: *I injured my wrist in 2009 and was no longer able to work as a cosmetologist, a profession I had practiced for twenty-three years. I lost my career and the use of my right hand at the same time. It was easy to fall into a deep hole of depression, and I did for a while. I thought, "Oh, why did this happen to me? Woe is me." Until I changed my negative thoughts to positive thoughts, I remained depressed. Instead, I began to think, "It's time for new beginnings. Something wonderful and new awaits me, and my life opens in new and beautiful ways that I cannot imagine for myself." Additionally, I searched the Scriptures, and Romans 8:31 stuck out: "What then shall we say to these things? If God is for us, who can be against us?" (NKJV). I internalized the verse; it became a mantra for me.*

  _____

  _____

  _____

- **Discussion:** How can we draw strength from our faith to overcome life's challenges?

_____

_____

_____

_____

Lesson 2: *Cultivating Positive Habits*

- **Objective:** Discuss how habits like gratitude and optimism can build resilience.

_____

_____

_____

_____

- **Activity:** *Gratitude Journal*
  Keep a daily gratitude journal for one week, reflecting on the blessings in your life. Example: *Be intentional about writing down how God is blessing you despite challenges. If you should happen to be without pen and paper, text that moment of gratitude to yourself or leave a voice memo on your phone. Capture the moment in a tangible way that will allow you to revisit that blessing.*

- **Reflection:** Discuss the role of *gratitude* in maintaining a resilient mindset.

_____

_____

_____

_____

Module 7: Nurturing Relationships

Scripture: Ephesians 4:31, 32 (NIV)
Get rid of all bitterness, rage and anger . . . . Be kind and compassionate to one another.

Lesson 1: *Social Support*

- **Objective:** Highlight the importance of healthy relationships and social support for a person's mental well-being. A healthy relationship is characterized by trust, respect, honest communication, and the ability to compromise and support one another.

_____

_____

_____

_____

- **Activity:** *Relationship Mapping*
  Map out your current support network to identify areas for growth. You will draw a square at the top center of a blank sheet of paper and put your name there. Draw a line and write the name of a person in your support network or community and consider ways to improve and evolve.

- **Discussion:** How can we cultivate positive, supportive relationships?

_____

_____

_____

Lesson 2: *Boundaries and Communication*

- **Objective:** Teach effective communication strategies for expressing needs and setting healthy boundaries, using clear and respectful language that communicates your needs. Example: *I appreciate your concern. However, I need some space.*

_____

_____

_____

_____

- **Activity:** *Boundary Setting Practice*
Practice assertive communication in a role-playing exercise.

- **Discussion:** How do we communicate our boundaries with love and respect?

_____

_____

_____

_____

Module 8: Self-compassion and Acceptance

Scripture: Colossians 3:12 (NIV)
. . . clothe yourselves with compassion, kindness, humility, gentleness and patience.

Lesson 1: *Practicing Self-Compassion*

- **Objective:** Define *self-compassion* and explore its role in emotional well-being. Example: *I approach challenges with kindness by speaking uplifting words to myself, fostering a mindset of self-compassion.*

  _____

  _____

  _____

  _____

- **Activity:** *Self-compassion Letter*
  Write a letter to yourself—offering kindness and compassion as you would to a friend in need.

  _____

  _____

  _____

  _____

  _____

  _____

  _____

- **Discussion:** How can self-compassion help us accept our imperfections and move forward with grace?

  _____

  _____

_____

_____

Lesson 2: *Acceptance and Letting Go*

- **Objective:** Explore the importance of surrendering to things beyond our control and embracing imperfection. Simply put, make
peace with what you cannot control because hanging on to it will
do more harm both physically and emotionally.

_____

_____

_____

_____

- **Activity:** *A "Letting Go" Ritual*
Engage in a symbolic activity (e.g., releasing a balloon or writing
and burning limiting beliefs) to represent letting go of past hurts.

- **Reflection:** How does our letting go allow us to grow in faith
and resilience?

_____

_____

_____

_____

Module 9: Sustaining Self-care Practices

Scripture: Mark 6:31a (ESV)
"Come away by yourselves to a desolate place and rest a while."

Lesson 1: *Creating Rituals*

- **Objective:** Learn to integrate self-care rituals into your daily, weekly, and monthly routines.

  _____

  _____

  _____

  _____

- **Activity:** *Self-care Ritual Creation*
  Create a personalized weekly ritual that incorporates various practices you have gained from this manual. Example: *Write a gratitude journal and incorporate mapping your resilience.*

- **Discussion:** How can rituals help us stay grounded in our self-care journey?

  _____

  _____

  _____

  _____

Lesson 2: *Monitoring Progress*

- **Objective:** Explore methods for tracking progress, for adjusting, and for celebrating small successes.

  _____

  _____

  _____

- **Activity:** *Progress Tracker*
  Create a visual tracker to monitor your self-care routines. Examples: *Journaling, app trackers, or calendars.*

  _____

  _____

  _____

  _____

- **Reflection:** How can you remain flexible and patient with yourself as you grow in your self-care practices?

  _____

  _____

  _____

  _____

Module 10: Reflection and Wrap-up

Scripture: Psalm 46:5 (NIV)
God is within her, she will not fall; God will help her at break of day.

Lesson 1: *Reviewing the Journey*

- **Objective:** Reflect on the growth and transformation experienced, and spiritual insights gained throughout the journey. Example: *What stood out the most that you will likely continue?*

  _____

  _____

  _____

- **Activity:** *Reflection Circle*
  Share stories of growth, challenges overcome, and lessons learned. Decide whether you will gather in one big group or multiple small groups.

  _____

  _____

  _____

- **Discussion:** What does it mean to be empowered through self-love and spiritual care?

  _____

  _____

  _____

Lesson 2: *Continuing the Practice*

- **Objective:** Be encouraged to continue your self-care journey beyond the curriculum.

- **Activity:** *Support Circle Commitment*
  Separate into accountability pairs or form small groups to provide continued support. Example: *Exchange information with someone in the class you can relate to and hold one another accountable.*

  _____

  _____

  _____

- **Reflection:** How can we maintain our commitment to growth and self-care in the long term?

  _____

  _____

  _____

Conclusion

As we close, I want to leave you with this sacred truth: She who is me, She who is you, is infinitely valuable. You are a vessel of wisdom, strength, and resilience. You carry the light of those who came before you, and within you flows the wisdom of generations—unshaken, unwavering, divine.

When we honor one another, we honor the legacy of Eve, the mother of all living. We honor the sacred wisdom that breathes within us, whispering courage in our moments of doubt, reminding us of our worth when the world tries to make us forget.

So, stand tall, Beloved. Walk in your power. Know that you are never alone. Wisdom walks beside you, within you, around you—guiding you, shaping you, calling you to rise into the fullness of the woman whom God created you to be.

With Peace, Love, and Gratitude

—Shevalle

www.ingramcontent.com/pod-product-compliance
Lightning Source LLC
Chambersburg PA
CBHW051248120626
46547CB00014B/1849